Owl
Poems

Owl
Poems

Zach Hively

Casa Urraca Press
A B I Q U I U

Set in Questa.

Author photographs by Magdalena Lily McCarson.

25 24 23 22   2 3 4 5 6 7

First edition

ISBN 978-1-956375-11-4

CASA URRACA PRESS

an imprint of Casa Urraca, Ltd.
PO Box 1119
Abiquiu, New Mexico 87510
casaurracapress.com

For Mags
and all you bring to life.

"I can't help but wonder how differently the land will smell when our children's children inhale; I can't help but wonder if they'll ache for something they don't know is missing."

−Laura Paskus,
from *At the Precipice:
New Mexico's Changing Climate*

Owl Poems

World-watching Owl,
    wielder of wisdom,
you death-dealing minder
    of midwinter moons
and summer monsoons,
    sniping silent prey while still
bewitchingly well-preened,
    keeper of chaos contained,
I call you: come,
    watch me at my work
as part of this world,
    you a bird apart, preordained.
Devour me in velvet tones,
    talons tussling at stanzas
and words winding their way
    within thirsty thoughts.
Bring me back a life
    born of breaking fasts
in far-off fields,
    feathers pulsing atop pines
because only you can know,
    you captor of cryptic simplicity,
how to untease the threads
    woven like intestines
into the necessities of both
    beginnings and ends.

The owl caught me between a wedding and a gravedigging. Too obvious not to have meaning. She flagged me down from the shoulder of I-25. Shouldn't be this flawless and this light and this dead on hot pavement. Nothing new, but this time out of all the times, all the times some creature ends up crumpled, she hooked me. Tugged me across the rumble strip, reeled me back against traffic. Her wing caught the roar of passing cars. Talons curled. Eyes closed. Feathers immaculate. She, perfect, in a world imperfect with windshields. I folded her wing back into her body. Her lifelessness secured that way, not so floppy, somehow. Shrouded her in brown packing paper, tucked her in the hatch with this month's recycling. Bore her home.

Bones keep appearing in the yard.
It rains?
    Boom—bone.

Wind blows?
Boom—bone.
    Fragments and pieces,

the intricacies
of dissolved marrow,
    and I wonder

how many creatures
resolve their lives
    in a tree

pinned to a limb
the way I secure a butternut
    to the cutting board,

tendons stretched
and snapped
    to sate

some ancient impulse
deep, deep in a raptor's
    breast.

Some say mice freeze
in the grass-seeded fields
when they hear the owl.

I froze in the sun. Dead,
she could have beckoned me
anywhere,

over the guardrail and
into the concrete ditch
spattered with goatheads,

sideways into traffic to
willingly embrace a big rig.
What else could I have done,

once thawed
by the same force
that froze me?

What good are abstract gods anyway?
I mean, hooked beaks are tearing open bellies
and flowers grow along the highway
and neck kisses melt into phantoms
like amputated limbs, gone.

Where are the gods of grass seeds,
of the promise that the clouds will unzip
eventually, of the coyotes
ignoring my dogs and the sin
of barbed wire?

I want the gods who can tear the rot
from my ribcage and stash scarlet
globemallow in the tooth marks. Give me
the gods who root their fleshy lips
on my thinnest skin.

I can believe more easily in a cottonwood
tree and a scraggled sage in a pile of mulch
because they too reach for the rain
and not for me, just a man left holding
an empty watering can.

If owls wrote poems
I think the haiku would be
much, much too wordy.

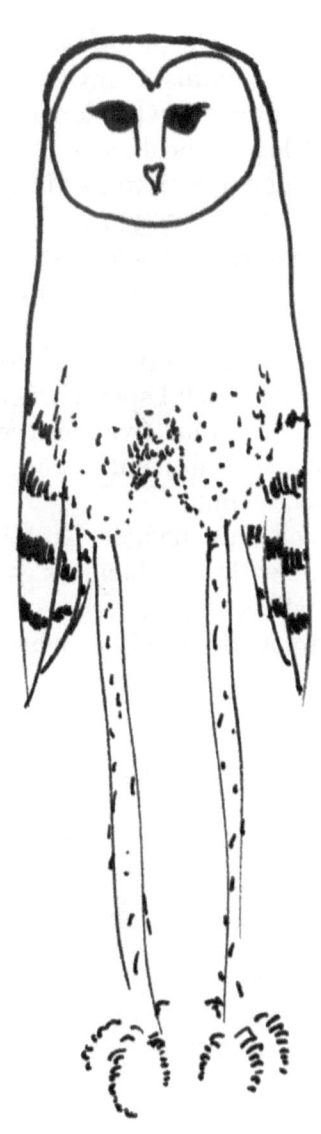

I might outlive the piñon forests
in these mountains, in my desert.
We are not meant to live longer
than whole swaths of trees.
Long enough to believe we always
have more time, enough of it to kill
some just to get through it, too much
to comprehend what it's worth.

My older dog can admire a pine stick
for an hour, which I spend begging
for him to stay four, five more years.
I cannot spoon him and swoon
    at his sleeping
without hearing the hole, like a flooding well,
he'll leave with me when he's gone.
And he will be—gone.
He knows it, and he chews a branch.

I know it, and I distract myself
trying to get a signal. Five more years
—a miracle for him, while I might
        yet outlive
the piñon forests in these mountains,
in our desert. Someday, I will want
to die, to leave my own hole, to answer
the owl, earn her trust, find myself
outlived by the trees we have left.

Four months of these winds
spare key uncovered from dust
still in plastic pouch.

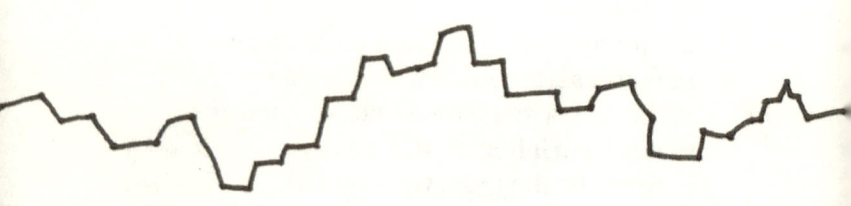

I cannot capture a sunset with a poem

any more than I can with a camera,

than I can suffocate it with chloroform

and pin it to a board.

Translation loses

so much of what

I have to say.

I hear you,
sometimes, at night,
when I stand with the dogs
and look for the galaxy
through the cracks
in the clouds.

It's been a while.
I try not to take it personally,
but it feels like it must be me,
too scattered, too
elsewhere, too
busy.

Call to me
on these muted nights
so I can shell myself,
drop the plating I carry
against both remembering
and forgetting.

I can't exist alone.
The prey, though in terror,
blood heated in a
last-ditch mad dash,
feels the thrill of being
chosen.

I don't want to run.
Quite the contrary.
I want to talk—
to listen to the owl's
five sultry notes,
over and over again.

The way a smooth stone
carries still water to my nerves.
The way a childhood book
brings comfort in the telling.
The way I would cut out
my own organs

on a night like this one
and put them back again
like clouds closing
over galaxies
just to take another
walk with you.

If I had it all,
everything as I dream it,
would I still want it?

Once, she brought me a taste
of what's to come.

Lifted away everything that
I think makes me me

not my tongue but
the words I breathe

not my toes but
the way they play

to soothe my nerves
not my eyes but

the light that bounces
around in them

She left me hearing
but without ground

(perhaps this we preserve
on the other side)

(for a bit, like someone
calling you, submerged,)

(to get out of the pool
before lightning grows closer)

She, though, like any great teacher,
gave me a chance to learn again

dropping me back
into myself

funny bone here
charlie horse there

all the someday-things
in their proper nooks where

I had stashed them
inside my skeleton

—calling from the telephone wire
draped along the street,

"Don't you dare, hoo hoo,
don't you dare forget."

Owls are bad luck in so many traditions they can't all be wrong. Messengers of death, ill omens. Do not touch. Yet I brought owl feathers into my home—senselessly still part of a whole dead owl. Didn't know what I was doing, just that something needed done and, well, there I was. Anything besides baking on an interstate. A body deserves better than asphalt. So—I laid her, paper shawl and all, like a hammock burrito when I was younger, in the coolest part of the house, in the bathtub. The right sacrilege for the moment. For once, I was fortunate not to belong to a people, to any tradition at all. No experience with what the world means. My people are not a people, just a bunch of people winging it.

Flowerpot in the driveway:
can't move it by my lonesome
so there it sits
right where it plopped
out the back of the truck

Cosmos and sunflower
with morning glories
twining their way up it:
I have the prettiest
driveway out of town

Honeybees swarmed me.
All my fault: I didn't ask
and I'm not the wind.

There's fluorite in these hills.
Worth as much as it's worth to me.

Just past the barbed wire—
all I have to do is cross it.

Pick a spot, crack a few rocks
just for the feel of it.

Even more fun if I don't get seen.
It's an invisible kind of work,

this breaking of everyday stones,
this conviction that there must be

something waiting for me to find it
and show it to the sun—

I've come all this way.
There just *has* to be.

The dog steals bunnies
from the bobcat's dusty cache
two days in a row.

When the one you love most
holds your hand to fall asleep
and you ache inside the complete
satisfaction of knowing just how
flawed the world still is.

This could all go away
any minute, could all crumble
tomorrow. You could never
fall asleep holding hands again,
not because everything is temporary

(which it is) but because
everything must be temporary.
Freedom is learning to stop
counting the licks left to the
tootsie-roll center of the tootsie pop.

You want to stay awake all night
to savor the hand-holding except that
the falling asleep is what you savor
the most about it—the ache *is* the joy,
the salt that perfects the sugar.

Whenever owls call
from junipers in the night
I hear you passing.

Creature of habit, inhabitant,
beast on land that doesn't need me
doesn't feed me—I eat bread off trucks
stomp scars in the crust
hoping hard to shrink my mark
like a good boy

Who am I to think I must tread lightly?
This is the goal of people who feel
—self-appointed stooges
of the campsite rule:
hold in our breath and hover over the dirt
until the earth hardly remembers we exist

Sometimes I wonder if my bones remember
how to swing from trees until, until, until
... my feet turn to rocks
and my arms to branches
and my senses slip together
      into other shapes
until more civilized folk
      can't tell the difference

The puppy dog chased a turkey vulture
this morning, disturbed its horaltic ritual
to get the blood pumping, pursued it
to two different cliff tops boom boom
overlooking the dry cobbled creek.
He gave up, came back, cliff not too high
but the bird too boring, refusing play.
You're too fresh, the vulture said
—written in air, plain as hieroglyphs—
too fresh for me, but I am patient,
have never starved yet.

I plant sunflowers.
Pack rats gnaw them down to stubs.
So I plant some more.

You should get an owl,
she said when the vermin
vandalized my ill-advised
plot to grow.

One with a swivel head.
So the plastic owl
lives on my fence, perched
on the rebar up its butt.

It watches over the
measly potatoes
and the one
remaining onion.

How does this work?
Does it? Rats are smart.
They feel. They plan.
Bunnies? Maybe not.

Not with real coyotes
to fear, real owls.
I cannot comprehend
how a decoy dummy

like this swivel-head owl
could ever deter
a hungry belly
now, in this drought.

Then I ask myself
why am I not doing
any of the things
I came back to life to do?

What stops me
half as real
as a plastic owl?
Nothing, of course!

Yet still
I wait
for the head
to turn away.

The poet writes: Trust—
the hardest discipline. Yeah?
Try trusting again.

The logic of lost loves:
I don't do all the things I could do,
because I did not do all the things
I could have done.

               The logic of not-yet loves:
            You must choose me for who you are,
                      and I you for who I am,
                            yet here we are.

The logic of being this age, unmarried,
childless, yet indescribably content, so happy
I could disintegrate like a sunset (except
when I'm not): There ain't no love like
     doggie-dog love.

                        The logic of owls:
                        Who-hoo,
                              hoo,
                        hoo hoo.

Shouldered a shovel to the gravedigging. The old man down the road chose, sometime between morning and not-morning, to cremate his dog's body. His knee was unhealed. He couldn't dig deep with a walker, not deep enough. We sat and talked instead, all the while a dead owl's body rested in my bath. Tradition is beyond me, it seems: a two-woman wedding in a courthouse after breakfast, a bodyless funeral before dinner, an owl choosing me to settle some business for her. Laid her in state on the kitchen counter, spoke secret and unskilled wishes over her remains. Gave what remained to the sand and the ants and whoever else would do their part to take her in, make her cells their cells, make her bones their bones. Took her death and made it mine.

dormir, schlafen, sleep:
when rolling off different tongues,
do dreams taste as sweet?

I'm all feather and predator
not quite content in this drought
until that flash of stiff ears
slides across sand
slides across my navel like
hunger doesn't even matter
—the thought salivating
not to tear after like my dog would
but to swoop in silent-like.

No bunny fluff
no gratuitous cute
all sinew and stretch
I've seen jackrabbits before
torn heart from chest
but never like this
—peel back the fur
nuzzle the flesh
sink a talon in fierce caress

wounding myself to dish
such a small death into
some greater breath.
I'm only human gnawing on cliché
as if less alive than this need
to pin myself to this creature
—to the earth's soft floor.
But the hare is in the sage now
and what I cannot catch

cannot claw
I pretend to dismiss as if
letting go is my choice.

A rattlesnake brings
you right back
to your skin.

Money-mind can't
account for three,
four feet of

weirdly green unspooled
to absorb maximum
bashful sun heat.

The spine knows
—only the spine
can shout through

the cud pinched
in the brain's
worn-smooth teeth

and shoot you
up a tree
—no tree, fine,

jump back then
put packed dirt
between you and

this easy giver
of liquid *no*
minding her own

on the road
that's not anymore,
all hers now,

sing her back
to sleep to
sing your own

electricity back into
your own bones
to prove yourself

no real challenger,
just some plebe,
interloping, clumsy, grateful

for life granted
promising to watch
your step, at

least a little
more, at least
a little longer.

Arroyo flowers.
Four summers I haven't seen.
Am I dormant too?

Georgia had a bomb shelter.
She listened to her friends in Los Alamos
plucked her model
      from the Sears, Roebuck catalogue
had it installed at her home on the hill.
It's falling apart, now,
      smells like a dead raccoon
and something more than that,
      something more, more.

This woman thought she could survive
      nuclear war indoors
when all the evidence suggests
      she would have withered up
preferred offering her bones
      to the radioactive sky
to bleach, flake, in sight of the mountain
      God gave her
so someone else could pluck her skull,
      preferred that
to living out her air supply with tins
      of dog biscuits.

Or maybe that's just me.

Two things remind me
that I live at the bottom
of an atmospheric ocean.

One: the hawk rasping.
Two: the junipers,
whatever else they're doing,
baking perfume in their bark.

I don't know why.
But these draw my howling bones
to surface, me a sentient
shipwrecked skeleton

choosing stillness with breath
free to flow, not held
any longer in open ribs,
happy to have the sun

splinter me one dry sliver
at a time, pluck me to pieces.
She loves me, she loves me...

Love. It might just be
handing you my bestest wings
trusting I'll still fly.

Burn the twigs:
crack branches to ash
the heat of turning
something to
nothing.

I think I should like
to be eaten,
shake shake
shake, moving
things along.

I want the best
even if that's simply
becoming a stack of parts
to sharpen beaks
and teeth on.

Could I ask more
for my own bones
in the end,
once beyond the pain
of fearing the end?

Fire and the alchemy
of being eaten—
the feat of turning
into nothing
is something.

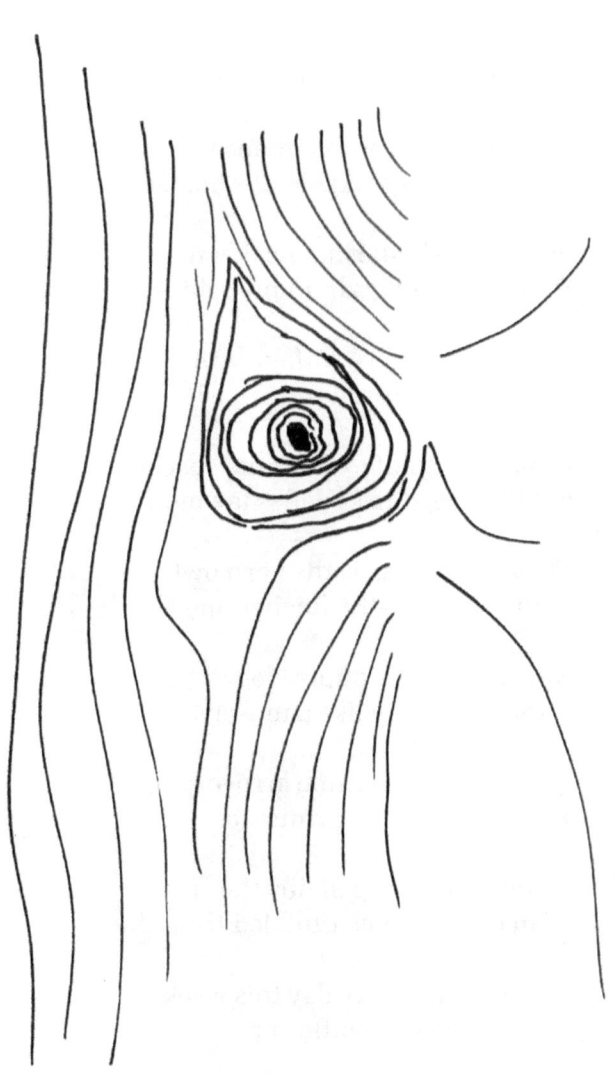

This can't be happenstance,
some chance of knots in sheets

of wood: the eyes too intense,
the tufts unmistakable, the bodies

of these owls staring me down
from the woodgrain in my cabinets

too alert, feathers ruffled with
dare I call it attitude.

Guidebooks fail to show me species
but the owlishness defies taxonomy.

They are, just as is the barn owl
in the arroyo—the further one,

whose walls the puppy dog
revels in scaling like a muscly

wolf spider. The same arroyo
where an evening primrose

rooted in a clump of dirt the size
of an engine block tumbled from the top

has bloomed every day this week,
one thick decadent flower

burning a month's ration of water
and white. Where one morning,

I was thinking about owls and how
I was too busy to write them letters,

something cracked a juniper twig
right over my head and my ancient

instincts sputtered and that owl
swooped, deservedly brash, to the

other side. If joy is the unifier
of life—and I cannot doubt

that it is—the cabinet owls are stern
only in their insistence that I

finish the dishes
and get *out* there already.

Return me to earth the way she had it, picked at and plucked, carried curiously under a juniper tree, pinned like a treasure map to the four corners: coyotes to the south, crows to the north, beetles to the west, everyone else to the east. Don't know how others like to die, but I sure know how I like to live—do unto others, such a sweet ideal—so in a clumsy way, my interloper way, bumbling like my opposable thumbs had been lopped off by a dull, rusty lack of ancestry in this place, without an origin story to light the world and my space in it, I do the most sacred thing I can: stack some rocks and let the owl and the earth, the nearest gods I know, decide.

The way before me
like a meadow in moonlight
after dry, dry snow.

An owl's blessing:

May your feet always be quick,
    because a chase is more fun.
May your breath always stay calm,
    betraying you to no one but me.
May your days fill themselves with bounty
    to layer sweet fat on your bones.
May you live serenely in the peace
    of forgetting what awaits you.
May you also remember always that the sun
    is not betrothed to the day.
A day will come, for you,
    that the day does not come for you.
May you rejoice in the knowledge
    that your flesh is an offering to me.
I will mantle my wings around you.
    All is not and never will be lost.

I am grateful to the early readers of these owl poems for their encouragement, their inspiration, and simply their presence: Magdalena Lily McCarson, Carol Ovenburg, River Stingray, and V. B. Price. Thank you all.

Marty: thank you for guiding me (or helping me guide myself) when the owl appeared.

I owe thanks as well to Jennifer Rife at the Laramie County Library for coordinating the *Habitat* book arts invitational, and to Mark Ritchie for curating the exhibit and collaborating with me on "More Civilized Folk"; his visual art incorporated an earlier version of one of these poems.

And, always and forever, I appreciate my dogs, Hawkeye and Ryzhik. They sat by me while I wrote each one of these. I owe them a walk right about now.

Z.H.

Zach Hively lives near Abiquiu, New Mexico. His second collection, *Desert Apocrypha*, received the Reading the West Book Award for poetry. His Fool's Gold humor column has earned three first-place awards from the Society of Professional Journalists' Top of the Rockies awards, and he has won a Maxwell Medallion from the Dog Writers' Association of America. He is also the author of *Wild Expectations*, with photography by Magdalena Lily McCarson. The two write music and perform together as the alt-folk duo Oxygen on Embers.

You can read selections and learn more at zachhively.com.

Casa Urraca Press publishes poetry, creative nonfiction, photography, and other works by authors we believe in. New Mexico and the US Southwest are rich in creative and literary talent, and the rest of the world deserves to experience our perspectives. So we champion books that belong in the conversation—books with the power, compassion, and variety to bring very different people closer together.

We are proudly centered in the high desert somewhere near Abiquiu, New Mexico. Visit us at casaurracapress.com for exquisite editions of our books and to register for workshops with our authors.

www.ingramcontent.com/pod-product-compliance
Lightning Source LLC
Chambersburg PA
CBHW031254120626
46545CB00007B/2803